# AT THE TABLE
## WITH
# JESUS

*A Collection of Insights with Impact*

## Miss Doddie

PUBLISHED BY BOLDER SPIRIT PUBLISHING

# BOLDER SPIRIT PUBLISHING

Designed by Roxanne Bellamy

Cover by Angie Alaya

Expressly edited for the preservation of the
authenticity of the voice of the author.

Edited

by

Roxanne Bellamy
Sharlyne C. Thomas

ISBN-13: **978-0692105528**

# Foreword

## by

## Mary Brotherton

When I was a teenager, there were days I felt I couldn't go on with the drama of being me, living the life I'd been given in a small, rural area of South Carolina. I thought nobody cared. Growing up in a large family, it was hard to get special attention from anyone, but I always knew if things were too much to bear, I could walk or run the half mile to my grandmother's house and she would make time for me. She always listened without judging or interrupting. Then, softly, quietly, she gave her sound advice. At the time, I didn't know I was hearing words of wisdom.

When I first started reading *At the Table with Jesus*, I didn't know how much wisdom would be packed in that little "travelin' book." Reading Miss Doddie's words felt like I'd run down to my Grandmomma's and sage advice from a wise woman. This book is written as I suspect the author speaks, with a homespun attitude, just like my rural grandmother's. Words that come from her heart, not from something she'd learned in a classroom. Words like, "Used to be with the drinkin', the more I drank, the more I wanted. Now I'm off that bottle and I'm on that Bible. Now I'm drunk off the Word, and boy does it feel good." The book, *At the Table with Jesus,* holds more than 150 little bits of wisdom and reading it feels like going home.

Mary Brotherton, President at **PEACECORE, Inc.** and Editor in Chief at **bUneke Magazine**, also runs her own editing business in Florida.

# Author Message

I give God all the glory! He changed my life and He wants to help you, too. I thank God for sending Roxanne my way to help me put this book together so you could see what God wants to do for you. This book is dedicated to you, the reader.

## *Welcome to the feast!*

### Miss Doddie

# Welcome to the feast!

**1. God's Word tastes good.** That's why you want more. You eat something, you feel good off it, so you keep on eating more. When you're at the table with Him and you eat more, you don't get overloaded, and you don't gain weight; you gain a clean heart.

---

**2. Do you know our spirit needs food?** I go shopping for food for my spirit. I go shopping in my book for scriptures. The Bible is groceries. The more I read, the happier I get. I go looking and shopping in the Bible. I just look from book to book to fit what I'm thinking about. Like shopping with your cart in the store, you are going to get filled up. And you don't hear the cash register going click-click. Why? It doesn't cost us nothing 'cause God already paid for it. If you don't believe it, don't bother going shopping. It won't work. You got to believe it for it to work. Reading the Word fills you up with the spirit of joy. Sometimes I have to get up and walk around my table, because I get happy... filled up! Get filled up and keep filling up!

3. You have to know something about Jesus. You can't just go by what other people are saying. You have to get that for yourself. No other people can do it; not preachers, not pastors, not any other people. *You have to get in that Bible, get into those words, and you swallow them down deep into your heart.* It's food. You got to feed yourself and get that food that helps you.

4. God wants us to know He is the Master who loves us and is always there for us no matter what we go through. We have to have a little something go on in our life so we can feel Him, so we can see Him, so we can know He was there. *If we stayed happy all the time, we wouldn't know He was there.* When we go through things and we get that pain, He'll take that pain away. Next thing you know, you'll get happy again. It's that knowin' about Him that helps you walk with a smile on your face. He's with ya.

5. If Jesus didn't have the heart He had while He was walkin' on this earth, we would all be lost. Even when He hung up on that cross, what did He say to God? "Forgive them for they know not what they do." That was that heart! We gotta

love HIM! ***How can we not love Him for what He did for us up on that cross?***

6. We need to know about God so we can get filled up and go out and gossip about Him. We need to keep in God's business and let it take over our mind and overflow from our mouth. That's how people can get fed. God will fill you up, and we got to let it out; otherwise, we will drown in it. ***God loves it when we get around and tell about Him.*** We don't have to be preaching. If you do it right, they want more. Before ya know it, they get overflowin' and they start gossiping, too.

**7. *We get our life together when we give it over to the Master.*** When we go to Him when we're going through, He'll give us a feeling.  And it's nothing but the Holy Spirit that will pick you up and help you stand tall. Go to Him. He's waitin' for ya and He got somethin' good waitin' for ya.

8. When you belong to God, somewhere along the way there's gonna be a light around you that other people can see. You don't even see it!  When people lookin' at you and they see the light, that light is helping someone. They see HIM! They will remember that light. It helps them see the way. The ones who seen the light on me, that wasn't me. That was Him. God used me so somebody else could see Him. ***He's got a plan for all of us to shine a light.*** Just get in the Bible. You'll see.

9. A lot of people say they're Christians, but they don't really know the way. You know what? A lot of people think because you are up in church constantly that you're a Christian. If you are doing it just for a show, then it's not it. God does not go for ones who want to show off for themselves. He gets the believer. The believer lives it. When we believe God and we are doing His work, we change. We change and it overflows. *We need to show HIM off!*

10. *When Jesus got up on that cross, God gave His heart.* He hung there looking down on us, looking all around for us. He was looking down so we could look up. He

does not forget us. He knows where we're at. He loved us and He loves us. We got to get to that package that was up on that cross. Pick up your package that was up on that tree. It'll take ya home. God is holding out His hand for us! THANK God. Thank HIM! He don't miss nothin'. That's what that cross was all about.

11. If you want to get to know Jesus, you got to let Him in. If you don't let Him in, you won't know Him. If you don't let Him in, He's like a stranger to you. If you don't let him in, He won't come in. He's not a burglar! *He's not breakin' in on you; He's waitin' on you.* He's waitin'. You got to LET Him IN! Let Him IN! He's got to come into our life so we can go back with Him 'cause He wants us back. He wants us to go with Him. He wants us in paradise with

Him! That's His LOVE. And that's what He came for.

12. The cross said it all. We got to have faith. Faith and belief go together. They are like a marriage to the Lord. God sees and He knows. He's gonna bring you through if you believe and trust in Him. It takes faith and belief; them two go together. He gonna do what He say He gonna do. 'Cause you know what? He's got everything we need. He said, "Ask and you shall receive," but you got to believe. ***There's no need to asking if you don't believe Him!***

13. You know, you got to be careful what you ask God for. You got to know what to ask for. God sees things that we don't see. God sees things that are none of anybody else's business. ***All you got to do is let Him in and He will work it out.*** Ask Him to do His will in your life and don't ya know, He'll do it.

14. People change. That's how come Jesus hung up there on the cross. He knows us better than we know ourselves. He knew we would change one day. He just waits. He has patience because He knew what we would be going through. God has a lot of patience. He doesn't want one of us lost. It's our decision... up to us to decide what we want to do. We have to pray. ***Talk to God.*** People change when we get in prayer with Jesus.

15. At one time, I was a show-off going to church and didn't even feel nothing. Puttin' my Bible down and lettin' it get dusty waiting to go back to show off some more. Now I'm puttin' the pages back together... wore my Bible OUT! I'm connected through the Bible. That's what kept me. It keeps me. **Reading the Word gets us connected and keeps us where we belong.** Get in the Word and stay in the Word.

16. We are all going out of here. God don't want none of us to get lost. We got to get cleaned up to go where He wants us to go out of here to. **We have to get washed.** We wash ourselves on the outside with

soap and water. God washes us on the inside with His blood. Sometimes when we go through all these trials and tribulations, that's Him cleaning us up on the inside. It's His washin' machine.

17. When you go to the store you have to spend something. God is different. The only thing you have to do is spend a little time with Him and you'll get the gift. Get still and open your heart and say, "THANK YA!" Things are going to change for you, but you got to spend some time with God. ***Spend a little time with that Master.*** Real joy is gonna show up for sure!

18. Christmas is a season. And there's a reason for it. It's not just about what is under the tree; it's what was hung up ON the tree. We get so busy with the presents and we forget about the present that was the Master. Thing about this gift is there's never no need to return it; won't need a receipt. ***Jesus is the best gift EVER, hung right up there on that old cross.***

19. You know what I love about ***Jesus***? He has patience with us. ***He don't get tired of us and just walk off and leave us.*** He stays. If anything, we walk off and leave HIM. He stays because He knows we need Him. He waits on us because He knows we're comin'. I get teared up. I get happy. This is what my tears are all about… joy… not sadness…JOY.

20. You know what else I love about *Jesus? He doesn't gossip.* When you tell Him something, He takes it to the Father and not to the streets. He doesn't gossip, but He likes it when we gossip about Him. That's not being false. That's the way the word gets around about Him and it's helping you, too. And the more you gossip about Him, the more He will give you to tell. Talk to Him as much as you can. And watch Him give ya somethin' to gossip about for sure.

21. Even though Jesus was raised up by a carpenter, He didn't just use nails and a hammer for buildin' and fixin'. He could do that, but He knew how to put us

together, too. That's what He came for. He came so we could get fixed. ***He used His body and blood so we could get fixed just right so we can go home.*** So WE can go. WE.

22. God uses the young as well as the old. God has workers and workers cannot sit down. ***We might get down for a little while, but God will lift us up.*** We need to know about God. Know how He works and He will use us more and more.

***23. Our life can be a spokesman for the Master.*** Our life can show off. Our life is showin' off God's power. Jesus got up and went down, but He came back up again. And He came up with all power. He knew what He had to do. He got that power to help us. He's still working. He'll never stop working. We just got to have eyes to see and know it's Him doing work in our life. God will lift us up again and again. Keep hangin' around Him. You'll see.

24. What we are goin' through, God is using for other people to see what He can do if we let Him in. And you gotta want to let Him in. If you don't want Him, it ain't gonna work. He knows... and He knows what we have to put away for a little while. He knows what we need to put down. *If we let Him in, put some things away, then other people can see Him.*

25. We all mess up in life. And God doesn't throw us away when we do. That's the reason why He got on that cross. ***Jesus didn't hang up there on the cross to save Himself!*** He got up there and gave Himself to save us! The reason it was done was to save us so we could get to Him through the cross. When we go to the cross, it's done and finished. He cleans us up! Nothin' else can do it, but the cross.

26. You know what? We have to bow ourselves to Him. Get down on our knees and believe. ***When we bow down, God knows we are ready.*** Bowing down. Get on your knees. Bowing down to the Master; it will set you free so you can get

to workin'. Lord knows we got a job to do 'cause He fixes us so we could go to work for Him.

27. God'll give you love, but it's not for you to keep for yourself. He gives it to you to share it. ***When you share the love that God gives you, it's got a feelin' to it.*** That's spreadin' that love that hung on the cross. BEST EVER! Can't beat it. No way, no way, just ain't no way!

28. God gives us time. He waits. He gave me time and it wasn't too late. We need to thank Him for letting us see what could have happened to us but didn't. We gotta

look at what we been through. ***Go out and see what He brought you from.*** See how He worked on you. Then thank Him.

29. We need to thank Him for being our friend 'cause we get to talk to Him. ***He's got a big ear for you.*** His ear, it belongs to you. He's got a lot of love for you and He loves hearin' from ya.

30. When you read THE WORD, whatever chapter you're in, you can see yourself in it. ***You can see yourself IN the Word!*** That's what brought me through and keepin' on keepin' on. Jesus – He is awesome. He is just awesome!

31. We can be thankful for the special place God meets us in our day. ***And we need to always be thankful that Jesus met us in His special place.*** His special place was right there up on that cross. He went there before us and waited for us to meet Him there. That's LOVE! And I just THANK Him!

***32. Jesus keeps His promises.*** Just know that He gonna do what He say He gonna do. He gonna do! All you got to do is just believe it. Believe it and He'll do it. You'll know it's true 'cause He'll show it to you. He'll show ya proof that He does what He says. He'll show ya.

### *33. That old Master, He's right on time!*
Hey, HEY, He's right on time! He knows what we need to learn and when we're ready to learn it. And how you gonna learn anything from the Lord if you don't go to the classroom? See Him comin' through a lesson learnin' in life… all kinds of lessons. Hang onto that old Master no matter what you're goin' through. He's comin' and He's right on time!

### *34. We all got a place in His place.* He'll give us the stuff we need to get in our place. I had to get in the right position to talk to the Master. It keeps me getting closer and closer to Him. I feel Him all around me in the daytime. You got to get in the right way to talk to Him, too. He knows what He wants to hear from you. So get in place. He's ready for ya.

35. When you talk to God, you talk to Him for the right reason... not for a greedy reason. Talk to Him about what you can do for Him, too. ***God will do things through you, not just for you.*** God gets us ready so He can use us to help other people. God makes us helpers, ya know.

***36. There's plenty of God to go around.*** That's why His arms were stretched out on that cross for all of us. They were stretched out, not folded up. His arms said "Come on in." And He wasn't looking up, He was looking down. He looked down. He was looking down at all of us. He had to look down to lift us up.

37. And when you talk to God and tell Him how you feel, He'll put somethin' in you. He'll put somethin' in you to help you and other people, too. And when He does, it will make you want to tell it! ***Don't be afraid to open your mouth for God.*** That's what He gave it to you for.

38. When you are workin' for the Lord, it might not be out of the house. It might be right there on the phone. People don't always have to see US. ***They need to see HIM in us.*** He gets into us so people can see Him. That's why we got to keep our mouth clean and watch the way we act. That way, we won't get in the way of them seeing HIM.

39. You know, the devil is busy. He'll have us thinkin' in ways that ain't right. He'll have you believin' that praying in secret is not a reward. You can't listen to him. Your prayers can be answered without sayin' it out loud. ***God sees what's in the heart.*** I didn't know, so I asked God for forgiveness for not praying. I shouldn't feel bad 'cause I didn't get up and hold hands and say a prayer 'cause I just didn't feel comfortable when I was just startin' out. I didn't have to get up and say a prayer out loud. I already prayed from my heart. Pray even if it's not out loud. The reward is comin' and it'll be you seeing Him come through.

40. Good Friday. Thinking about what it means to me. What it means to me? It means LOVE. I call it Good because Jesus loved me so much to hang up on that cross for me. That's Good Friday, because Good Friday is the day that we all became saved if we want to accept it. He said it was already done there on the cross. Paid in full. Finished. I thank God for it. That's what Good Friday is for me. I love Him. I thank Him. ***Good Friday is LOVE!***

41. The Master has been totally, totally good to me. He brings me joy. I love that Master. He's my friend. He's my best friend. Nobody knows what He has brought me through. Nobody... nobody. He wants to bring you through whatever it is, too. He will do it if you let Him. ***Spend some time in the Word and get to***

***know Him.*** Just can't tell it all. You're just gonna have to try it for yourself.

42. God's joy is the best when you are IN your mess. But when you're goin' through somethin', it seems like you just can't get it  because you're tryin' to figure it out. This is when you give it to God and He'll help you through it. His joy surrounds you all the way through it. All we got to do is talk to Him. ***He loves it when we talk to Him***. We have a lot of things that we need to talk to Him about. And one thing about it, He don't shut you out. He's right there... right there in it with you. Yes, He is!

***43. Jesus - He gave us a highway to God and you don't have to pay to get on it.***

You don't have to pay 'cause He already made the way. He paid for us. He paid it on the cross. We don't even have to have gas. Only thing we need is faith in Him and obedience to His Word and we'll be on our way on that highway home.

**44. You know, He was there before you got there.** Wherever you are, He sees you there and He sees you coming. If you don't believe it, look at the cross. Everything we needed hung right there on that cross. All you have to do is believe. Then you get happy. Even when things are around you making you stressed, God will fix it so you can get through it. He'll give you JOY! That's what He does!

45. Can you imagine how He gets happy? He gets all happy when He sees us coming home. Not your "Homecoming" when you die, you're coming home today! Coming home helps us on our way to that "Homegoing" one day. ***You are gonna have a new address.*** Your ticket has already been paid. Every day, you are getting closer and closer to going home. So get yourself together. Get yourself in order 'cause you are coming home! You're going home to Him right here, right now. Don't wait.

46. I had to go through something to get something from the Lord. Because you know when we think we got it all, we don't call on Him. We don't because we don't think we need Him. ***You got to let Him know that you know that you know who He is.*** You got to let Him know that you know He's got what you need. Then

you gotta get to Him. He loves it when you call on Him. He's your friend!

47. Jesus is LOVE! Jesus is a gift from God. God loved us enough to send His Son to hang up on a cross for us. *He didn't get up there and stay up there for no reason.* That was LOVE! Love hung on the cross for us. We just got to get to the cross and get what God has for us. It's a gift that's just waiting for us to pick it up.

48. His Word, His Word, His Word IS Him. His Word is in us and He is the Word! The living Word... the written Word is in us. He uses us for the living Word. His Word will not go back void. *God's Word does not die.* It will grow in us and it will cause

us to grow in Him. His Word is food... food for our spirit.

49. We gotta get into relationship with God. ***When we have a relationship with God He puts us together.*** God shows up through us and He puts people together. He is with us and He uses us so other people can see Him. We're all traveling together on our way home. If we don't show up along the way how are people gonna see Him?

50. I just look up in the stars and I thank God. I tell Him, "I see you, God!" He made all this. He made all US, too. We are all different colors and when you put us all

together, what a beautiful bouquet. ***God made us different colors for a reason... not to pick on each other.*** Some people, they might not say anything, but they will remember things... things they heard people say, or things people did. Think about it. He put us together 'cause we are a bouquet. And God loves flowers. He loves every flower He ever made.

***51. God's got feelings!*** If He didn't have feelings, He wouldn't have had His Son to do what He did for us. Now you tell me He don't have feelings. He knew we were gonna be in a mess. God knew the devil was out here and He sent Jesus to save us. He did it because He loves us. Sure, God's got feelings, too!

**52. God's got stuff for you.** You don't know what you're gettin' from God if you don't know Him. How you gonna really know what's from Him and what it's comin' for? You gotta know the one who is sendin' it. If you know He's sending it, you can trust it. If you know Him, you'll know what came from Him and what didn't. He's just awesome!

**53. God didn't leave us guessin'... He gave us a book to help with that.** The Bible is a book of understandin', but you've got to believe it so you can get understandin' about the things you need to know. That book... it's a helper. Get in it and stay in it.

54. Our mouth was meant for praisin' Him. How you gonna do that with a filthy mouth? You can't praise Him with that. I know. I had one. ***God uses your mouth.*** We have to watch the things that come out of it. We have to watch the things that go into it, too. When those tears were streaming down my face, He was cleaning out my mouth. I didn't even have to ask Him to clean my mouth. He knew what He needed to do so He could use me. He'll help you if you want Him to.

55. I used to be a drunk... not a drinker, a DRUNK! And how can I talk about the Master and I'm still doing the same thing? I don't want to live just any kind of way

no more. I'm alright just the way I am without that drinkin' since October 8th, 1983. That was the day I got a new life. I don't even have no taste for it no more ever since that day. ***He took me off the bottle and onto the Bible.*** See how He'll help you?  He'll help you even with what you're puttin' in your mouth.

56. I put Jesus in front. That's what He wants. He wants to be up front. ***When He got up on that cross, He didn't say, "Cover me up. Take me down."*** He stayed up there in front of everyone. He went up there because He wanted to. He stayed up there because He loves us. You know, that's some kind of love.

57. He is a forgiving God, but we have to remember who He is. We have to remember who we are, too. God changes us if we want it. *One thing about it is you can't try to hide what you used to be.* If people don't know how you used to be, how they gonna see what God can do? When you start talking about Him and you're all messed up, it don't draw nobody. You start talking about Him when you're cleaned up and on your way, and somebody gonna want to know about Him for them, too. That's doing God's work. That's workin' for Him.

58. God makes promises. God keeps His promises. He said He will not leave you nor forsake you. You know what I like about the Master? We might not feel Him all the time or see Him all the time, but

He's always with us and He's right on time. ***He's hangin' around us just like He said He would.*** We need to make it a point to hang around Him, too. Thinkin' about Him, talkin' to Him, readin' His book, and talkin' about Him. That's hangin' around HIM. That's just what that is. He likes that.

59. Take more time reading the Word, and the Word will get in you. It comes to you and it is all around you. You can feel it. You can feel Him. ***The more you learn about Him and the more you talk about Him, the heavier you feel about Him.*** That heavy feeling is joy. That heavy feeling brings tears to your eyes. It's joy!

60. You know, God has a place for all to go, but there's sides. I'm on His side. My knees got me there. My prayers got me there. I know what I'm talkin' about. I just love Him. I just LOVE Him! **He wants all of us to go with Him.** We just gotta make up our mind who we want to go with.

**61. Troubles make you hungry for God!** God already knows what you need and that's why Jesus got up on the cross! That was God being there for the needy. God is there with you. We go through some stuff to get to some stuff. We need to thank Him. Lord, I just want to thank you for my life not working out right so that I would truly want YOU in my life.

62. Sometimes the devil will use your hurt to hold you. The devil will put people in your way to keep you down to keep you close to him. ***God comes right on in to help you up when you ask Him, but you gotta want Him.*** That's when He comes in and helps you. He sure won't barge in on ya, though. You gotta invite Him.

63. You have to have peace with God. You have to have peace between you and Him. You got to know He'll give you peace if you'll accept it. ***He's a giver, not a beggar.*** You get that peace when you believe what He said He would do for you. You just gotta know that if you believe God, you will have more peace.

64. You'll see what God is doing in your life. While He's cleaning up, we straighten up! Then other people gonna see it, too. That's what God wants. *He wants people to see what HE can do.*

65. When we walk, God is using us 'cause you don't know who you gonna pass. Somebody can be feeling bad. You can look right at 'em and give 'em a smile. When we walk by someone we don't even know and give 'em that smile, that gives JOY! *God gave you that smile that you givin' to them.* We are working for the Lord! That makes God have joy. He gets joy when He sees what joy comes when we serve Him.

66. 'Cause Jesus did all the work on the cross we get to have assignments from God. Even though that part of the work is already done we still get assignments. It's our part. **Work the assignments.** And the more we work, the bigger our pay gets. Our pay is not silver and gold, our pay is for heaven. Our pay is for when we get there. That's where we goin', and that's where God wants all of us to be goin'!

67. Put Him first in all things and you won't be last... because He said so. Our God is all about justice. He makes things right. *He's not just gonna leave you in a place you don't belong when you put Him where He belongs.*

68. At Christmastime people put presents under the tree. We do it because we love each other. God gave us a gift because He loves us. He gave us Jesus. And Jesus didn't go under the tree, He went up ON the tree. ***Jesus was UP ON the tree, and He stayed there because He loves us!***

69. When we talk with Jesus, we got to feel comfortable. We got to feel comfortable for real. When we're comfortable with Jesus, that shows we love Him. You can tell Him and you can show Him. And they all work together. ***Just invite Him in, get quiet, and hang around Him for a while.***

70. When we go to God, He wants us to see Him. *When He got up on that cross, He wasn't all covered up.* He was stripped down. The more they did to Him, the stronger He got for us. So I love Him, I LOVE HIM, I LOVE HIM. He loves us so much, so much. He did what He did, because He wants us to see Him, so we can come in!

**71. God didn't say we HAD to come in.** We come in 'cause we want to and that's where we get happy. We get happy off it because we WANT to go to Him, not because we HAVE to. We get happy 'cause HE gets happy when we want Him.

**72. Jesus went out of His way so He could show us the way to Him.** You can talk to Him any time and any place. It don't have to be a certain place. You can just talk to Him. I went to Him and He give me that joy. And that joy was so great, I just keep on going back to Him for more. This kind of joy in my heart don't never go away... because He's there. You can get Him, too. Get Him deep in your heart and in your spirit. God's Word will hug you. That kind of hug will keep you going back and won't never run out.

73. We get peace and joy when we talk to Him. Just His name gives joy when you call on Him. It keeps buildin' up. He listens to us when we can't sleep and we just need to talk to Him. **He don't never sleep and He's always there to listen.**

He's right there ready to listen. Just talk to Him. It'll make you feel good.

74. We have to talk to Him about Him, too, not just about us. **We have to tell God we know something about HIM, too.** When you get into Him and get into the Word, you will know more about Him. He already knows all about us, but He still wants to hear from us, too.

75. God doesn't want confusion. He straightens out things. Listen for Him; He's talkin'. **He's talkin' to you to help you.** He fixes things. He wants to help you fix things. You won't be confused if you

listen to Him and do what He says. You can trust Him. That's for sure!

76. You know things will come your way and it's a surprise? That's God givin' to ya 'cause God loves to give gifts. ***That cross had a gift for life.*** It was love that hung up on that cross. Go to the cross and talk to Him. That's what it's all about. He didn't have to do it, but He did it! Go ahead and talk to God.

77. When we listen to Him and He tells us to do something and we do it, God gets happy. ***God gets happy, too!*** This is where the joy comes from. The Lord gets

happy with us because we listen to Him. He gets joy, too. HE gets joy, TOO!

78. If everything comes my way, how much would I pray? Somethings just can't always be easy. **We can't just stay comfortable.** When things aren't easy, we go to God and He helps us along the way. He wants to hear from us to help us along the way. Let Him do it.

79. God's got it all and He wants to give it to us. We just need to get there. It didn't cost us nothing. Only thing it costs us is to believe and we shall receive. **He's got**

***power for what we need.*** He's more than enough power.

80. God has ears and His ears are to hear. His ears are for you. He loves it when we talk to Him. And He loves to hear us talk about what He has done. So go to Him and put Him in it. ***Tell Him how you feel about HIM.*** Don't you think that'll make Him feel good, too?

81. Love don't carry no hurt! Because when Jesus got up there on that cross, He took all that pain. He took all that pain and He STAYED up on that cross because of love. He did it so we wouldn't have to

carry that pain no more. And that love He has for us don't go away. *Love don't go down, it stays up; just like He didn't come down off that cross.* He didn't come down. He stayed up there. He stayed up there because of LOVE!

82. When we listen to Him and we don't keep it to ourselves, then we get it out where it belongs. That's how God's working with us. And when He works with us, His Word can get out. He uses us. He uses us to get His Word out! So we got to listen and then tell it. But not just tell it, we gotta do it. *Do whatever He says.* That's how God's Word gets around.

83. You know we don't live alone? I learned this because I'm talking. I'm talking to Him and the thing about it is, He's talking to me. God's my company. He's not only my friend, He's my company. ***He's the best company you can have.*** What you tell Him, He won't tell anybody else. And He stays with you all the time. He don't never leave us alone. He's with us no matter where we go. He's right beside us. Me and God, we walk hand and hand together because we are meant to stay together.

***84. God don't never sleep.*** He don't want to sleep because He's got children down here. And He's watching us and taking care of us all the time. We just need to know that God is with us. And know who it is that is watching over us. Sometimes I might fall asleep talking to Him, but He don't never fall asleep listening to me. And I KNOW He won't fall asleep listening to you either.

85. Assignments. We got a lot of assignments for God. We can't just stop after one. God's not going to give you just one assignment. If He did, a lot of us would be lost. ***The more assignments we have in life, the more we learn.*** I'm glad that God didn't look down on us for one assignment. We NEED learnin'. That learnin' is what gets us where He wants us. He wants the best for us. He loves us. He's our Father!

86. God's eyes and His ears work together! He sees us and He hears us. *He seen us when He went to the cross and He heard us when He was hangin' on the cross.* That was love hangin'! We had to SEE that love He had for us when He hung there. It was nothin' but LOVE. He's waiting for us. And we have to decide if we want Him. We just got to get to Him. He wants us all!

*87. God even talks to us when we're sleeping.* How? Because He tells us when to wake up. If He didn't tell us to wake up, we wouldn't get up. We wouldn't get up because we wouldn't hear Him. He wakes us up and gives us a new day each day. This is why it's good to listen to Him.

88. Hope you picked up your Christmas gift from God! If not, it's not too late. It's waiting for you. Jesus was born and went back home. He hung on the tree for us. ***Jesus was born to hang on that cross so we can be born to go back home, too.*** It's the only gift that makes everything right. Just get to the cross. You're not too late. Jesus waits for us to come to Him. He sees you coming and He waits. That's love!

89. Sometimes we need to look back at all we went through and then look at us now. ***We need to remember what God did for us.*** We go through something so people can see. A lot of people can talk about something, but God shows through our

body what He can do 'cause our body talks, too. Our body talks, too, so people can see what He can do. Our body does not lie. Our mouth sometimes can make mistakes, but our body does not lie. So I don't mind what I went through with that stroke. God carried me through and showed what He can do!

90. God fixes our mouth so He can use us. Our words are God's beauty. It's God in us that shows in our ways. ***God didn't just get in us to just sit there.*** He put His beauty in us to work for Him. Things can get rough, but we got to think before we open up our mouth and let our tongue get rough. The devil is right there waiting to grab our mouth and use it. When God's in us right, we don't want to hear that rough

mouth stuff and we don't want to speak it. How can we talk both ways?

91. We have to ask ourselves, how much do we know about Jesus? Are we goin' by what somebody else says or what He says? When you know Jesus, really know Jesus, you get joy. Unspeakable joy! *That kind of joy, you can't explain it; you just show it!* Get in the Book, get to know Jesus, and get in His joy!

92. On Memorial Day, we remember the ones who went to fight and died so we could have a better life on this earth. We need to be thankful... very thankful. And

how about Jesus? *He died so we could have the best life forever with Him.* God made it work for us. That work on the cross was what made it work. His blood is our weapon. It defeats the enemy!

**93. God loves it when we talk to Him!** He didn't tell us how many times we can come to Him. Just go to Him any time… not just when we're in trouble… not just when we need somethin'. But go to Him and thank Him for stuff. Go to Him and give Him some thanks. Give Him some praise. When you do, He loves that!

94. You know, you can think about God in different ways. God is a tree. The tree is strong. This tree is strong and the roots are deep. It stands through the storms even when the winds knock the branches off. During your storm, you hang onto that tree. ***When you are in  a storm, you got to look up, keep ahold, and keep on moving.*** You go through stuff, but don't get off that tree! Grab ahold of that tree and look up. That tree helps you look up.

95. You know the devil is out here and he's got eyes on us? BIG ones! The devil doesn't want us to see Jesus. And don't you know God's eye is way bigger than the devil's? God knew the devil would be looking for us, tryin' to get us to go with him. That's why God sent Jesus. We just have to look up. ***Don't look down, just***

*look up and see Jesus.* See Jesus on that tree. He got up on that tree because He sees you and He doesn't want to lose you. He hung on that tree not because He had to, but because He wanted to.

**96. We really need to be sure we understand that God has an ear for us.** He hears us and He gives us everything we need to make it through the hard things in life. People go through trials and tribulations and when you go to Him and talk to Him, His ears are open to every problem that there is. His ear is a healer. I still thank Him for what He brought me out of... for getting me right and fixin' me so He can use me. That's how I know He's got an ear. He fixed me. And He keeps fixin' me. You think He don't have an ear for you, too?

97. When we have Jesus in our life, we don't have to talk about it all the time. You know why? Because it shows up. And the reason why it shows up is 'cause He shows up, and He's right on TIME! *We just have to carry Him in our heart and He'll show through.* He'll show through right on time.

98. God'll give ya an ear like His if you ask Him. When I start talkin' to Him, I get that good feeling 'cause I know He's listening. I know He's listening, 'cause it gives me joy. His ear gives me joy! We need to have that same kind of ear. *We need that ear that heals and gives joy.* People need to feel it when they talk to us. We need that helpin'

ear for people around us like His helpin'
ear for us.

99. I just wanna take this time to thank
God for giving me my ticket for my way
home. I'm riding that train home and I got
my ticket hanging there from that tree.
The tree that Jesus hung on for me is
where I went to get that ticket, and it
didn't cost me a thing. He paid for it. He
loves me. I know He loves me because
He's always with me. He's got a ticket
there for you, too. Get your ticket and get
to know Him. *He LOVES YA!* That's why
He got up there on that cross, so we could
be with Him. He wants to be with us.

100. You know there's a difference between hearing and listening? God speaks to us because we listen. Why? Because when we listen it sticks! And when we listen to Him and we understand Him, that's what makes us grow. And the more we listen, the more He will give us. The more we listen, the more we can help other people listen. *He wants us all to grow and make our way to Him.* That's LOVE!

101. Talking to Him is what gets our heart right with the Lord, and our spirit right with the Lord. When we get to talking with God, we feel peace. We get peace. God gave this to us when Jesus went up on the cross. He made the way for us to go talk with the Father. *It cost Jesus His life,*

***and it don't cost us nothing but a little bit of time.*** That's the truth.

102. How are people going to know what He's all about if we don't open our mouth and talk about Him? When you have God in you, things will come out that are right for other people, too. The more we open up our mouths, the more He'll give us to talk about. Open up your mouth for the Lord! ***Gossip about Him!*** We gossip about the worldly stuff, now let's gossip about the spiritual stuff.

103. You know what? Jesus has got everything already! We just got to tell

Him what we know... what we know, we know. ***We just got to go to Jesus and leave it alone!*** All we have to do is accept Him because He is the one who brought everything to our heavenly Father. We've got to go to Jesus and talk to God. The two go together.

104. Now I see why I had to fall apart 'cause if I hadn't, I wouldn't have Jesus in my life. All the bumps and bruises from our life get smoothed out because we WANT it. A lot of times, we say we have to have it, have to have it, have to have. We have to WANT a relationship with Jesus! ***Jesus is just waiting for us to invite Him into our life.*** He waits for us because He LOVES us!

105. Reading the Bible sometimes, I just have to cry. One morning, I felt like someone was just hanging on me. I said, "I know this is You." I was talking to God just like that. "I can tell by Your touch; the touch of love," I told the Lord. I said, "You had to be hung up so I could get up. And I just want to thank ya." **He hung up there and He hangs on us!**

**106. Jesus is a gentleman!** He won't break into your life. He'll knock and wait for you to invite Him in. He waits for you. How do I know? He waited for me. It took me some time to get to Him. You know why He waited? He waited because He knew I was coming. He'll wait if we need Him to.

107. We can look at the Word and it will only do so much. You can't just look at it. You have to digest it. When you chew on His Word and you digest it right, you get filled up. You get hungry again because you like that taste and that keeps you wanting more. ***Ya gotta stay hungry to go back for more.***

108. You know, we are like flashlights. We are in a world of darkness and we are the light. Sometimes we might feel out of place. When we are in a crowd, we have

to be careful 'cause sometimes we feel like our light is dim. That's when we need to get in the Word. ***God's Word helps us get more light.*** That's because God's Word IS the light that gets inside of us when we read His Word.

109. How you gonna learn anything from the Lord if you don't go to the classroom? We got to get in God's light. That's where the learnin' is. God lets you see things in the darkness when you are using the right light. We are going to see things different now 'cause we are learning from that light He shines. ***When we are in God's light, God's light is in us.*** It brightens things up.

110. We got to put out some stuff and get other stuff in. When you are going through something and someone says things that hurt you, and it makes you feel bad... makes you feel down, you just got to think about Jesus. That helps to put out stuff. You got to think. When you start feelin' down, think about the Word and it lifts you up, puts stuff in, and heals ya. ***God's Word is a healer for our wounds.***

111. Jesus hears your prayers. He hears you talkin' to Him. He had ears for us all when He got up on that cross. ***You got to believe.*** No sense in talkin' to Him if you don't believe! Faith is something that you grow into. You got to get to it first for it to grow. Just get to the cross. He hears you.

112. The Bible... the way it's worded, it don't hurt people. This is where gossip comes in. People get out here with words and it hurts you, but ***God's words don't hurt you; it's LOVE. It fixes you.***

113. Time is winding up and people need help. ***We all need help.*** That's why I get on my knees and tell Him, "Here I AM! I'm here again. I want to thank you, God, for letting me in. Thank you, Lord, for the cross that opened the door so we could get in where You want us to be!"

114. Keep readin' the Word and you will understand more and more. The more you read, the more you see. The more you see, the more you will receive. ***Your eyes see so your heart can receive.*** Keep feeding your heart. It will help you grow and get you strong like God wants to you be. He wants your heart to be strong for Him. Keep readin' the Word.

115. When you and God have a good connection, He can trust you. He trusts you, so He tells you more. When He tells you more, you learn more. ***Learnin' keeps us going in the right way, doin' things the right way.*** When God has something He wants us to do, He's there with it, too. Yeah. When He looked down at us, He knew what He needed us to do. He looked down knowin', and we need to look up to Him believin'.

116. I love talking to the Master, because I know He's my friend. He doesn't run away when He sees me coming. And He's right there to show me the way. And I didn't have to keep on asking Him. He was right there waiting so He could see me through. I just love Him! He's waiting there for you, too. ***You don't have to get dressed up to talk to Him.*** You can talk to Him just as you are 'cause God dresses up our spirit. Our spirit gets dressed up by His Word, and you don't look out of place.

117. God made me a talker so I could talk about Him. He knows what He is telling me is not gonna get wasted. He knows it goes to helping... not wasting. He tells us things to help us. ***He tells us things to help other people.*** Me talkin' about Him is workin' for the Lord. It's my

assignment 'cause I for asked it. I asked for that assignment 'cause I wanted it. It came quicker to me because I wanted it. I ain't got to look for a job; my job is right here serving the Lord.

118. When we listen to God and follow what He says, that's how life gets better. Things get better for you and better for the ones around you. Sure, it gets hard makin' it through sometimes, but you gotta believe God. *He sees us down here.* He knows when we want to get better. Don't you think He wants us to get better, too? He sees. He cares. Talk to Him and listen to Him. Read that Bible and do what He says. You'll see.

119. When you talk to God, you gotta listen for His answer. God tells you things because you listen to Him. His words are not wasted on you. *God don't waste His words.* That's why He loves talking to you when He knows you're listening. Why is He gonna keep talking to someone who won't listen? God don't waste. He'll wait. He'll wait 'til you're ready to listen.

*120. That relationship with God, it grows.* You gotta water it. It needs that water to grow. The Word is water. It waters your spirit. It helps you grow to be closer to Him. That's that connection... like roots. He wants us to have that connection with Him. He wants us to be close to Him. When we get in the Bible, He's in that Word. He meets you right there in the Word. That's why we gotta keep in the Word. It's feedin' ya. You gotta get in it and sit with Him for a while.

121. God knows you want to hear from Him. You gotta want to hear from Him. You gotta want to. He knows we need it, but you still gotta want it, too. When you open your mouth to God to ask Him somethin', open your ears, too. That's how it works. ***Your ears and your mouth go together when you're serving the Lord.***

122. God's got time, but make sure you're on time. We serve the Lord because we ask Him what we can do for Him. That's how we get assignments as His workers.

*God's got time alright, but we need to make sure we get with His time.* When we work with Him like this here, He gives us more to do. He sees what we're doing.

123. Look around and see God all around ya. He's all around you. If you don't see Him, you'll feel Him. Sometimes we can see where He's at, and sometimes we can feel where He's at. We can see and we can feel. He's everywhere. *He's everywhere because this all belongs to Him.*

124. God is our Father and we are His kids. Don't it make sense that He wants us to grow? He wants us strong and healthy.

He loves us! Why wouldn't He want us to grow? And if He wants you to grow, He'll give ya what ya need. He won't leave you on your own. *His love keeps us strong and His Word is food to our soul.*

125. You know your heart and your eyes, they go together? You can see with your heart. When you feel things, God is showin' you something. Pay attention to your heart. It's a classroom for learnin' what we need to learn. *God is a teacher.* That's why Jesus comes into your heart.

**126. God wants you to be seasonin', you know.** He wants you to make life taste good to people around you. He puts those people there. He puts them there and He gives you a job to do. He calls you to be salt while you're here on this earth. We got to spread His Word. When you spread His Word, don't add to it and don't take from it, and it will be seasoned just right.

127. People around us feel our ways. They feel our ways and they feed off our ways. That's why we gotta watch our ways and do the best we can. ***God wants us to be a help.*** We can't do it on our own. Good thing God is a helper. He'll help ya do it if you ask. You work together with Him. And when you're workin' for Him, it makes life good for you, too.

128. God does the cleanin'. You still gotta ask for it though. ***You gotta go and ask for the cleanin'.*** He'll come right into your heart and sweep out all that stuff that's keeping you back. He'll clean it right outta ya. That cross was His broom, ya know. He was cleanin' with that cross. And His blood is what He washes us with. He did it all right there on that cross. All the cleaning and all the supplies were right up there on that old tree. All we gotta do is go to that cross. You gotta go to Him. He'll do it. You just gotta get there. The rest of it is already done.

129. God is a healer. He fixes things. He wants you to come in, so He fixes it so you can. He'll even hold the door for you, but you can't wait too long. It can be too late. Don't wait too long 'cause we never know

when our time is up. ***Don't wait 'til it's last minute and your time is winding' up.*** He wants us to come in NOW so He can help us through what's right here. His help is for here, too, not just when you leave outta this place. He's not just waitin' for you to get there. You know He's here for you right now, too?

130. God wants you to get on board that train home. He wants you to come home to be with Him. It doesn't cost you a thing. Your ticket is already paid for. ***He's got everything set and all ready for you.*** He knows that you're coming home to Him and that's why He's got your room ready for you to come in.  And we don't have to knock when we get there.

131. When you listen to God, He listens to you. It goes both ways, ya know. It's like opening up the road so you can get through to where ya belong. It's a two-way street. *He can come to us and we can go to Him... all because of that cross.*

132. God gives freely. *When He gives, He don't have to count, afraid He's gonna run out.* It's already been counted. God owns everything there is... and it's FREE! It's free to us that want it.

133. God sees us and hears our prayers, and the devil knows it. When I turned my life over to the Master, my whole life was turned around. You see what God has done for me. This is God's hand that is holdin' me up. ***God's got big hands and they're stretched out for you, too.*** He's just waiting for us to take ahold of it. God's hands will make you strong. You take ahold of it and don't let go.

134. I'm so thankful I don't have to beg for the things I need. I didn't say I don't need things; I said I don't have to beg for things. God takes care of me and sends people to help me out along the way. That's because God fixes things. When He fixed me and my attitude, He fixed the hearts He would use to help me when I need it. ***God is awesome... He just is!***

135. Jesus is the best friend you can ever have. We don't have to do a thing to have Him visit us. **We don't have to get all cleaned up to let Him in our house.** He's not coming in expecting everything to be all shiny. He's not looking for dust or checking your floors. If He expected the cleanin' to be already done before He got there, He wouldn't have had to get up on that cross!

136. The devil comes around and stirs stuff up being busy, but it just gets me closer to the Lord and I get happy. It's what God does for me that makes me happy. **God's joy and our happiness, they go together.** And when you got both of

them, it makes you just fill up and overflow. That old devil thinks he's hurtin' us, but he's really helpin' us to get closer to the Lord. Talk to God, put that devil under your foot, and keep on moving up.

137. Readin' the Bible, sometimes you got to keep searching and reading, searching and reading. You gotta go looking and looking in different parts to get that full understandin'... almost like shopping in the grocery store, goin' down all those different aisles to get what you came for. Even then, there are times when you gotta ask God about it, too. **When you searched and you still can't get it, ask Him to help you see it.** It's not easy sometimes, but just keep at it. Talk to God while you're

readin' and He'll show ya the way. He's right there with ya.

138. I think about where I come from and where I'm at right now. I think about where I'm leaving and going to. That gives me joy right there, just thinking about it; and I ain't even got there yet. This right here is just for now, but our home with Him is forever. That's where we need to keep our minds at. **We need to stay focused on getting to that forever home.**

**139. God's got a train comin' for us.** I'm not going to be too late 'cause God got me right on time when I got down on my knees. That's when He brought that ticket to me. That ticket comes with believing and obedience. Obedience is the key. It is not to destroy; it's to lift you up to go home. Obedience is the taste of life. It's not bitter, it's sweet. It's the taste of everlasting life with HIM!

140. That cross is the way home. *You know God made a road when Jesus got up on that cross for us?* That road, it's not like the old road you were on. Once you get on that new road, start traveling that road. When you do, that's when you see a difference in your life. And the thing about it is, you get on that new road and you don't even want to look back. Looking back don't even sound good no more. You want to go forward. You wanna go forward with Him 'cause you feel it and

you know it. He's taking us someplace good 'cause we wanna be with Him.

141. When I'm outside, and people just come to me, there's something that they see in me. Some of them don't even know who I am, but they know who I am serving; otherwise, they wouldn't stop by. People will see the Master in you. ***When you stay close to Him, you start lookin' and actin' in ways that show Him.*** He rubs off on ya!

142. I might have a little hurt, a little pain, or whatever, but I'm still healthy. I'm healthy because I got Jesus in me. And He

took all that pain when He got up there on that cross. That was medicine right there. He was holdin' my pain. I don't have nowhere near the pain He took for me. ***That pain that He took on the cross set us free.*** Now that's love!

143. If I ask Him for something, and I don't get it, it's because I must not have needed it. God's not gonna give you something that might be a harm for you in some way.  He loves you. He holds things back because He loves you. ***He's the best Father there could ever be.*** So trust Him and thank Him when you don't get what you asked for 'cause then you know you didn't need it.

144. I don't' have to wait until daytime to talk to God. Why? 'Cause He's right there all the time. You can't interrupt God. He's waitin' on ya. He's got His ear out for your voice. He knows the way you sound. *He made that voice you have.* Use it with Him. And when you do, you gotta believe He's there for you. If we don't believe He's there for us, why are we askin'?

145. That old devil wants you to think. Thinkin' about the wrong stuff is a trap. Our thinkin' too much is what can keep us from growin'. It keeps us stuck. *But God will help you if you're stuck.* That's why I'm always talking to the Master, 'cause that's where my help comes from. He's right there with the answer, all you got to do is ask for it. He will put a light on what it is you need to know. God's voice will

keep us out of the devil's way if we listen to it the right way. Listen and do what the Master says.

146. People need to eat. People that don't have food can go to a place that will feed them. You can go to a place where you don't have to put money down to buy something. You can go there, eat freely, and then leave... no begging needed. And when you leave, you feel alright and you'll come back. It's just like feeding on the Word. People need a place to eat for the spirit, too. ***Spirit gotta be fed.*** You can go to the Bible, and eat from it freely, and you're welcome back anytime!

147. You can look at the Bible in a lot of ways that help you to stay in it. It can help you if you want to stay in it. You don't have to... that's up to you. It's a decision you make. When you want to, He starts showing you all kinds of things in that Book. Everything fits together from the beginning to the end. You have to be patient. That Book if FULL of stuff to change your life. ***The Word changes you and when it does, here comes the glory.***

148.  When you go to cook something, you get out the recipe book to see what you have to have where you can make it right.  You need to know what goes in for it to come out right. When I get in that Bible, it's like baking. That Bible is a recipe book. It gives us all the ingredients

right there. ***Do what the recipe says, and it will be alright.***

149. God knows what we don't know. He sees what we don't see. He's higher than we are. He's The FATHER and He knows what we need to know; that's why He talks to us. ***His words are a helper.*** And we don't have to pay nothin'; all we have to do is pay attention. We pay attention because we want to know.

150. Some people come right up to me and it's just like we been knowin' each other for years, and it's my first time seein' them. I understand why, though.

They talk healthy. It's familiar. I know who they're serving. I can tell who they serve. I can tell... tell by the way they are. We're connected by the One we are serving. **We're related through Christ.**

151. I'm not sitting at that Bible to make myself look good, it's to make myself feel good. We feel good when we do things His way. He feels good so we feel good, too! It's not so people see me readin'; it's about what's on the inside, not the outside. That Word is left with us to go on the inside of us. God gave us His Word so we can get healed, get strong, grow, and have that joy. **In that Bible, them words are not just words; that's life in them words.** We gotta get that down deep inside of us. That's what makes us what He wants us to be.

152. Sometimes I'm reading the Word and it don't even sound right. I don't understand it. The Bible's not always easy for me to read, but I have to keep going. It has different parts that all come together. If you are thinking, thinking, and thinking, "Did I get it right? Did I get it right?" That means you got to keep going. When I keep going over and over because I don't understand, I keep searching until it feels right. That's when I know I got it right. I can feel it. **God's Word has feelings.** His voice has feelings. God's Word makes us feel good. It makes us feel happy. It makes us feel joyful.

153. You know the devil is busy out here showin' up tryin' to mess us up. There's times when I mess up and I want to get cleaned up. That's when I need to go back to God so I can get cleaned up. I'm not perfect. When I get talking and I feel myself going astray, I just tell God, "Get that devil out of my way." If I was perfect, Jesus wouldn't have had to hang on that cross. He hung up there so we could get connected to God. *God knew we were gonna have trouble; He knew we'd need His help.* We all do!

154. Just because you decide to go along with Jesus don't mean things are gonna be easy. Nope, it don't mean that at all. What it means is you won't be lost and you won't be alone. *When you go through, Jesus goes every step with you.* He's

behind ya and in front of ya. He knows where to go and He knows how to get there. Once you get Him down in you, He won't never leave you. Never. We can walk away from Him, but He won't walk away from us.

**155. If you want to get cleaned up on the inside, call up Jesus.** You don't have to pay for that call. He always answers. He's never too busy for you. He won't say "You gotta make an appointment." He'll come on in when you call Him and He'll do all the cleanin'. He'll clean your mouth, your mind, your heart... EVERYTHING, if you want Him to. We can't do that kind of cleanin' ourselves. Only He can, and He won't send you a bill neither. It's PAID in full already. He paid the price for your cleanin' forever. It's already done.

# AT THE TABLE WITH JESUS

# Author Reflection

I can't even explain how it feels to have God use me. There's so much grace and mercy in it. He knew what He was doing. He was watching me all along. He was with me. He never left me. He knew I wasn't gonna leave once I got it right. I wasn't gonna  leave and not do it. This is why I'm working for Him where people can see what He can do for them. He uses us so people can see. He does it 'cause He knows we'll talk about it.

I'm not gonna deny it. I'm not proud of being a drunk - a DRUNK, not just a drinker. But I'm not gonna keep it from people knowin' what I was. Used to be with the drinkin', the more I drank, the more I wanted. Now I'm off that bottle and I'm on that Bible. Now I'm drunk off the Word, and boy does it feel good.

I'm not staggerin', I'm readin'. This is where I get my happiness. I get filled up with the Word. The more I read it, the more I want to read it.

God is just awesome. He's awesome. I can't even explain it. The only thing I can say is, "Thank you to the Father, the Son, and the Holy Spirit." All three of them showed up together.

That cross has taken all my worries away. I know when I go, I know where I'm goin'. I believe in Him. That's the main thing. ***You gotta believe in Him, then obey Him.*** He loves ya!

# About the Author

Miss Doddie wants you to know that "God is REAL" and God has brought her a "mighty long way." As she would say, ***"God does clean-up and I'm proof of it!"*** In the darkest hour of her struggle with alcoholism, she got down on her knees and prayed to God to fix her so He could use her. That is exactly what He has done. She says that was the day she was given a new life. For decades now, she lives completely free from "the bottle."

Daily, her heart is full of gratitude for how God took her "from the bottle to the Bible." Every morning, she sits in the very same spot at her kitchen table, reading from her well-worn Bible. There she consistently enjoys "feasting on the Word at the table with Jesus" until she is filled to overflowing.

Miss Doddie is committed to spreading the word. Time and time again, you'll hear her say, "Look what God did for me!" The heart God has for her is the very same heart God has for you.

Photo by Craig Grant

Now Miss Doddie invites you to dig into *At the Table with Jesus* and feast on the very same insights that have spiritually fed her and kept her for years.

# God bless!

Photo by Craig Grant

*Miss Doddie*

95179727R00067

Made in the USA
Columbia, SC
07 May 2018